THE ADVENTURES OF
Sella + Ella

"ONE RAINY DAY"

written & illustrated by Gabriella & Marisella

First hardcover edition January 2021

Written by Gabriella Albano and Marisella Mercado
Illustrated by Marisella Mercado

ISBN 978-0-578-82091-0

Published by Ellahaus Publishing
www.EllahausPublishing.com

In loving memory of our beautiful mother,
in whom we owe our imaginations,
creativity, and treasured bond of sisterhood.

And to our dear baby sister,
who came into the world much later in life,
but brought an increase of laughter,
memories, and sisterly love with her.

Meet Ella and her sister, Sella,
who follows her in every way.
They share parents and adventures
and even shoes on some days.

But which sister is which?
Well, that's no trouble at all.
Sella is little
and Ella is tall.

To see what adventures
the girls are on today,
just turn the page
and follow them
along the way...

One Spring day, the sun
was shining and warm.

The girls were heading out
to play when...

"Look!" yelled Ella.
"It looks like a storm!"

Yes, indeed a storm
was heading their way;
bringing thunder and lightening,
the rain pouring away.

"Oh boo," cried Sella.
"There goes all of our fun!"

"Not so fast," assured Ella.
"The fun has only begun!"

"Come with me," Ella said,
"and see what we can create!

We only need our imaginations
to build something great!"

"Look, Sella, a Castle!
With walls so strong and tall.

Do you see the dragons? Take up
your sword...

...we can conquer them all!"

19

"Come see! A plane!
It looks ready to fly!
Grab your goggles little Sella...

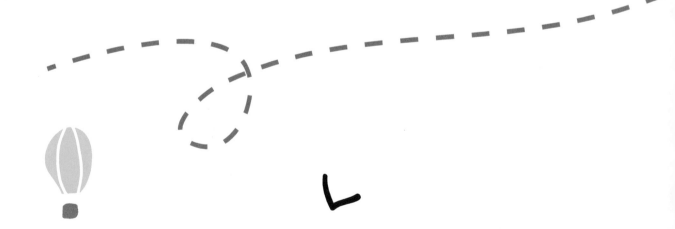

...let's meet the birds in the sky!"

"Or we can be astronauts,
floating high amongst the stars.
Racing our super fast rocket ships...

...around Pluto and Mars."

"Next, we can go camping!
Let's put up a tent, and
lay our sleeping bags on the floor.

We can tell stories as we
roast marshmallows...

...and eat hundreds of s'mores!"

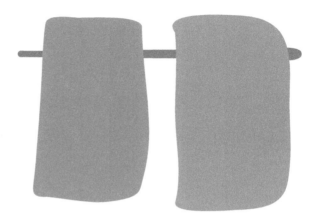

"Finally, let's go to the beach,
jump in the waves and lay on the shore.
Discover shipwrecks and treasures...

...and find coves to explore."

"I hope it rains tomorrow,"
yawned Sella as they got
into bed.

"It sure will be fun to see
what new adventures
we can find," Ella said.

The rain continued to pour as Sella and Ella slipped off to sleep.

They dreamed of
dragons and airplanes
and...astronaut sheep?!

So don't fret if the rainclouds come
and rain on your fun. Turn on your
imagination and get ready for the
fun has only begun.

Can you help us find Lucy?

Lucy is Sella and Ella's butterfly friend.
She is always flying near the girls in each adventure
from beginning to end.

Can you count how many Lucy's are in the book?
Flip through the pages again and have a look!

About the Authors

Gabriella "Ella" and Marisella "Sella" are two sisters who went on a lot of adventures together as little girls in San Diego, California. They were always together, allowing them to create great adventures both indoors and outdoors, taking them from the real world into a dream world of their own. They knew how to take a dull moment and turn it into an adventure-filled experience.

"Sella" & "Ella"

Now located in Texas with little ones of their own, they know how important memories, adventures, and the use of the imagination are to a child. The Adventures of Sella and Ella stems from these adventures. Combining their memories and their imaginations, they long to honor not only their history but also every kids' childhood, friendships, and relationships between siblings, and remind everyone what a little imagination is capable of.

Their hope is that parents, kids, and families everywhere find joy in taking part in these adventures, learning to use their own imagination, and creating adventures of their own.